Devon's Railway Heritage

Robert Hesketh

Bossiney Books

This reprint 2018. First published 2014 by
Bossiney Books Ltd, 67 West Busk Lane, Otley, LS21 3LY
www.bossineybooks.com
© 2014 Robert Hesketh   All rights reserved
ISBN 978-1-906474-45-4

Acknowledgements
The map is by Graham Hallowell.
All photographs are by the author. (www.roberthesketh.co.uk)
Printed by R Booth Ltd, Penryn, Cornwall

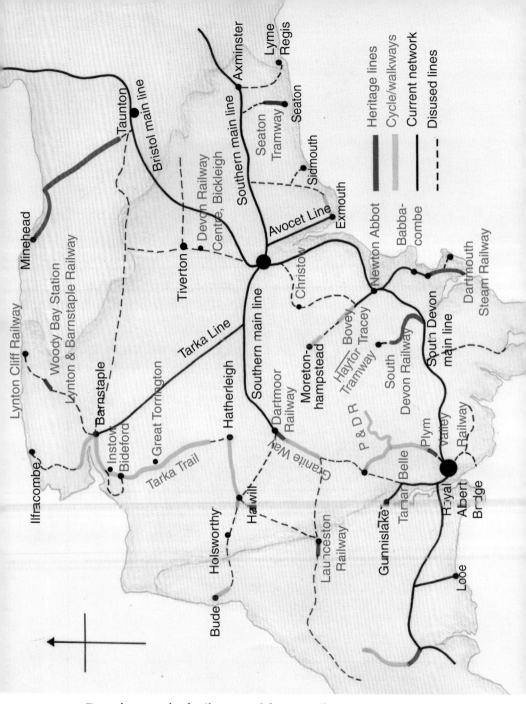

Devon's network of railways and former railways

The South Devon main line, heading out of Teignmouth

Introduction

From its early horse-powered tramways, through Victorian expansion to later contraction, then revival through preserved lines, railways have profoundly altered Devon, leaving a rich and varied heritage. This concise guide explores that heritage, giving practical directions and telephone numbers for railways and railway sites to visit.

In Devon, the railways' impact has been greatest and most durable in making seaside holidays popular and affordable, establishing tourism as the county's leading industry and rapidly expanding its coastal resorts. Through an extensive network that brought Devon closer to the industrial and commercial centre of England, railways made almost all this large and diverse county easily accessible and opened it to outside influence as never before.

Although that network was greatly reduced, especially after the Beeching Report of 1963, Devon retains its two main lines and four very attractive branch lines, plus a fine collection of preserved railways where vintage locomotives and rolling stock are complemented by meticulously restored stations. Devon's growing network of cycle/walkways using previously abandoned lines offers another way to discover the county's remarkable railway history.

Haytor Granite Tramway near the Haytor quarries

Devon's earliest railways

Built in the early 19th century, Devon's first railways (more properly tramways) served several quarries and mines. They used horse traction and were not part of a network. The most impressive is Haytor Granite Tramway, opened in 1820. It used granite rails and ran downhill 394 m (1300 ft) to waiting barges on the canal at Teigngrace, 13.6 km (8½ miles) distant. Long sections can be traced on foot by following the Templer Way (page 38).

Devon's first iron railway, the Plymouth & Dartmoor, linked Swell Tor and Foggintor quarries with Plymouth's Sutton Pool and Princetown by 1826. It climbed 424 m (1399 ft) through a meandering 41km (26 miles), and was converted to standard gauge in 1883. The Yelverton to Princetown section was re-launched as the Princetown Railway and carried traffic until 1956. Much of it is now a cycle/walkway (page 38).

Further examples of Devon's early tramways include Zeal Tor Tramway, built in 1846 on southern Dartmoor and the inclined plane at Morwellham in the Tamar Valley. Built in 1812, the tramway on Plymouth Breakwater connected with barges bearing trucks on rails – Britain's first train ferry.

The sea wall near Teignmouth on the south Devon main line

The National Railway Network

The main line to Bristol and London Paddington

Mainline steam trains burst into Devon for the first time in 1844 when the westward extension of the Bristol & Exeter Railway reached Exeter. A new era had arrived with the new line engineered by the dynamic and brilliant Isambard Kingdom Brunel.

Daniel Gooch, Brunel's talented locomotive engineer, drove the train on the first round trip from London Paddington to Exeter in one day – taking only four hours and forty minutes on the return. At an average speed of 41.5 mph, this performance was then unparalleled for sustained high speed running and a triumph for Brunel's 7 ft 0 1/4 in (approximately 2.14 m) broad gauge system.

Regular services to Paddington were scheduled at only five hours, including stops, making them the fastest trains in the world. Stage coaches such as the *Telegraph*, which had amazed passengers by reaching London in a mere seventeen bone-shaking hours only a generation before, could not hope to compete. Neither, for most purposes, could canals such as the Grand Western for bulk transport.

Railways changed our awareness of time. Midday in Plymouth is actually more than 16 minutes later than in London, and in coaching days clocks used to be set to local time. The Great Western Railway (GWR) was most affected because predominantly an east-west route and found these local variations unworkable, so in November 1840 it adopted standardised 'railway time' – effectively London time. Every station had at least one prominent clock – complemented by the station master's prized watch and chain. Once the railways arrived, timekeeping and timetables became part of daily life.

Track building followed at a whirlwind pace. The railway reached Teignmouth in 1846 and thrust forward via Newton Abbot and

A steam excursion train hauled by LNER Class A4 4-6-2 'Union of South Africa' leaving Dawlish Warren

The south Devon main line near the Hole Head tunnel, east of Teignmouth

Totnes to Laira (Plymouth) in 1848, thus completing in a mere four and a half years what is still Devon's premier main line and its most vital connection to the national network.

Devon's hilly terrain and many rivers make the achievements of Brunel and his army of navvies all the more remarkable. The line they built with muscle and rudimentary mechanical aids continues to give travellers an impressive and wonderfully scenic entrée to the county.

Brunel overcame his first major obstacle, the Blackdown Hills on the Somerset border, with the 992 m (1092 yd) long Whiteball Tunnel near Culmstock, but the Haldon Hills were an even more formidable barrier. His bold solution was to follow the Exe estuary and thence the coast to Teignmouth via five cliff tunnels and a 6.5 km (4 mile) long sea wall. The line has needed frequent repairs against the ravages of the sea ever since and is sometimes closed during storms.

Scrapping his next idea of routing the South Devon main line

Brunel's Atmospheric Railway

Brunel's controlling and inspiring influence is apparent all along the South Devon mainline, but with his atmospheric railway of 1847/48 he over-reached himself. Surviving pumping houses at Totnes and Starcross stations are souvenirs of this ingenious but short-lived experiment, which is also recalled at the Atmospheric Railway Inn opposite Starcross station.

The Atmospheric Railway was designed to bring speed and efficiency to the difficult and hilly terrain west of Exeter by replacing locomotives with stationary steam pumping engines. These created a vacuum in a central pipe that ran between the rails and was joined to the train by a hinged piston, thus drawing it along by atmospheric pressure. The concept of generating power outside the train and thus reducing its weight dramatically was perfectly sound: late in the 19th century electric underground and mainline trains would make it viable.

Brunel argued that the cost of pipes and stationary steam engines along the line would be more than offset by savings in other directions. The trains would be far lighter without their heavy (and costly) locomotives, thus less fuel and lighter, cheaper rails could be used. Lighter trains would cope better with steep gradients and be cleaner and quieter too. In brief, Brunel was fascinated with the apparent potential of this technology, which had been applied with some success on short lines elsewhere.

The atmospheric system only operated from September 1847 to June 1848 between Exeter and Newton Abbot. It never reached Totnes, although the pipes were laid. At the beginning, its performance was promising. Speeds of over 60 mph were attained, but in the winter the all-important leather flap valve, which sealed the continuous slot along the top of the pipe, often froze; rats gnawed it and the salt air completed its destruction. Costly repairs were required. The pumping houses used far more fuel than expected.Uncoupling steam locomotives at Exeter and substituting carriages with atmospheric pistons was time-consuming and labour intensive. Making junctions with other railway lines and accommodating level crossings presented major challenges.

Starcross Station, with its atmospheric railway engine house, topped by a flag

via Dartmouth to Plymouth, Brunel settled on the present shorter route along Dartmoor's southern edge. This avoided the massive engineering challenges posed by crossing the Dart estuary and some of the steepest gradients in the South Hams. However, the terrain west of Newton Abbot demanded several expensive works, notably the 'South Devon Banks'. These four exhausting inclines include Dainton Bank, at 1:38 the third steepest in mainland Britain. Until well into the diesel age, the South Devon Banks placed constraints upon the length of trains or called for more powerful or additional locomotives.

Brunel's bridges

Brunel courageously admitted his error of judgement. He introduced locomotives forthwith, scrapping the project that had so enthused him. The Atmospheric Railway was a financial disaster. Brunel partly redeemed himself with the railway company by building a remarkable series of economical timber viaducts. Five Brunel timber viaducts spanned the steep valleys between Exeter and Plymouth. There were seven more on the line between Plymouth and Tavistock and two on the Newton to Kingswear line. Taking the railway westward from Plymouth to Penzance demanded fifty-one more timber viaducts.

Brunel designed his viaducts so that timbers could be replaced without closing the line. Specialised and highly skilled bridge repair gangs patrolled the West Country. Not one viaduct failed – a tribute to the durable, cheap Baltic yellow pine Brunel insisted on. Eventually, the supplies failed. Other timbers were tried, but none matched it. By 1883, stone, brick or iron had replaced all the timber viaducts on the South Devon main line. In several places, including the Ivybridge Viaduct on the main line (shown below) and the Cann Viaduct in the Plym Valley, the stone piers of Brunel's original timber viaducts remain near the structures that replaced them.

Royal Albert Bridge, Saltash

Brunel's 667 m (2188 ft) long Royal Albert Bridge was one of his greatest and most enduring triumphs. It still carries mainline trains (far heavier than those of 1859) over the Tamar – a tribute both to Brunel's skill in using bold and experimental technology and his wise choice of corrosion-resistant wrought iron.

The railway reached Plymouth in 1848 and met a major obstacle – the Tamar. Brunel's choice lay between a steam ferry at Torpoint, and a bridge at Saltash. Here the river narrows to 300 m (1100 ft) and rock outcrops provide some solid support, though in parts they lie 20 m (70 ft) below mud on the riverbed, as Brunel found when he conducted his usual meticulous survey – 175 trial borings in this case.

He decided on two great trusses consisting of oval tubes in the form of a parabolic arch, with the ends tied by two pairs of suspension chains, one on each side of the tube. The tubes are 140 m (461 ft) long, whilst the total weight of each span, including the trusses and deck, is 1060 tonnes.

All told, the Saltash Bridge took six years to complete and was a massive engineering feat. The central pier alone took three and a half years and involved working at pressure below the water level. Photographs show the incredible toil of raising the great spans in 140 lifts of 3 ft each – a task that took thirteen months.

The 'Torbay Express' pulled by GWR Castle Class 4-6-0 'Nunney Castle' (with a modern diesel locomotive assisting) at Newton Abbot station

Newton Abbot and its GWR Museum

The railway reached Newton Abbot in 1846, rapidly transforming it from a small market town to a key junction and an industrial centre with locomotive works and repair sheds. These employed over 1000 people in 1930. They closed in 1981, but remain as part of the Brunel Industrial Estate.

Newton Abbot is still an important railway town of special interest to researchers. Newton Abbot Museum (2a St Paul's Road, 01392 384700) has a host of railway artifacts, including a section of pipe from the atmospheric railway, scale model locomotives, engine name plates, lamps, pressure gauges, shovels and tools, the working parts from Newton West Signal Box and audio recordings of men and engines from the steam age. The Library (Market Street 01392 384012) has an extensive railway reference book collection including sections devoted to specific Devon railways. It also holds railway DVDs and a range of railway magazines.

Honiton Station on the old LSWR main line

The Southern main line into Devon

The London & South Western Railway (LSWR) opened its line from London Waterloo to Exeter in 1860. This gave Devon its second, more southerly, connection with the capital via Salisbury. It also linked East Devon to the burgeoning national network with principal stations at Honiton and Axminster, and made possible later branch lines to Exmouth, Seaton, Sidmouth, Budleigh Salterton and Lyme Regis.

LSWR's new line also highlighted a major problem which was not resolved for over thirty years. The railway employed the widely used 4 ft 8 1/2 in (1.44 m) gauge track (then called 'narrow' and later 'standard') championed by pioneering Newcastle engineers George and Robert Stephenson, with locomotives and rolling stock to match.

Laying a third track within Brunel's broad gauge on some Devon lines only partially solved the quandary of two systems. The inescapable logic of standardisation throughout the national network eventually triumphed and all remaining GWR broad gauge track was converted to 'standard' during one frenetic weekend in May 1892.

'Goliath', a GWR 5205 Class 2-8-0T built in 1923, steaming out of Churston

Devon's branch railways

Despite the 'war of the gauges', a plethora of competing railway companies and a lack of any coordinating body or railway strategy, Devon gained an increasingly dense network of branch lines through the 19th century and early 20th centuries, carried on a tide of rapid growth in the national and local economy. 'Railway mania', the speculative boom of the 1840s, came and went, but before Brunel died in 1859, the North Devon Railway was completed to Barnstaple (1854). Tiverton and Torquay had already been connected in 1848. Tavistock followed in 1858 and Paignton in 1859.

Development continued piecemeal, with lines snaking into ever remoter corners of the county and bringing Railway Age speed and rapid communications in their wake. Railway construction in Devon finally ceased in 1925, when the 33 km (20.5 mile) line between Torrington and Halwill was completed. Only remote Hartland in the north-west corner of the county was left beyond easy reach of the railway.

Railways and mass tourism.

Railways brought a population explosion to several Devon towns, especially resorts and junctions. Torquay had 8000 inhabitants in 1841, but 34,000 in 1901. Similarly, Exmouth's population rose four-fold from 5000 to 21,000 in the same period. Newton Abbot grew more than three-fold. By contrast, the county's total population only increased from 567,000 to 661,000.

Top: Goodrington's development began when the railway reached Paignton. Later the railway ran along the back of the beach, as it still does.

Below: Ilfracombe, a historic port, began to develop as a resort before the railway: its visitors arrived by boat, but the railway speeded its growth dramatically. At the peak of its popularity in the 1950s, 10,000 visitors arrived by rail every Saturday in summer.

Exmouth, Dawlish, Torquay, Budleigh Salterton, Sidmouth and Teignmouth had begun to develop before the railway arrived, but this was on a modest scale, and largely confined to the leisured classes. Two generations later, the new rail network transformed British seaside holidays. Cheap rail travel opened the Devon coasts to ordinary people for the first time, making previously exclusive resorts popular family destinations, especially as paid holidays became more common.

South Devon's resorts gained their railway connections early and expanded accordingly. The railway reached Dawlish and Teignmouth in 1846, Torquay in 1848 and Paignton in 1859. East Devon followed suit. Exmouth gained its railway connection in 1861; Seaton followed in 1868, Sidmouth in 1874 and Budleigh Salterton in 1897.

In 1874 Ilfracombe became the first North Devon railway resort. Lynton followed in 1898 and Westward Ho! in 1901. Despite this late start, North Devon's resorts grew in response to the railway stimulus and Ilfracombe gained a great heritage of High Victorian architecture to rival Torquay's. Its population stood at 3,677 in 1851, but reached 8,557 in 1901.

Contraction of the Devon network

Although Westward Ho! lost its railway after wartime requisition of its rolling stock in 1917 and the Lynton to Barnstaple line closed in 1935, it was not until the 1950s that Devon was deeply affected by line closures. Rising competition from road transport, both private cars and road freight (backed by a strong industrial and political lobby), combined with the neglect and lack of investment suffered by the whole railway network during the Second World War made many branch lines unprofitable.

Through the 1960s and 1970s Devon's track mileage dwindled further as branches were closed. Services were reduced and many halts and stations were shut too, notably on the main line between Totnes and Plymouth and between Exeter and Taunton – though the new Tiverton Parkway station (1984) and a new station opened at Ivybridge in 1994 were some compensation.

Closure of the line from Barnstaple to Torrington and Meeth in 1982 marked the end of network contraction. Devon was left with the former GWR main line and the former LSWR (later Southern Railway) main line, complemented by the surviving branch lines.

The Riviera Line connects at Paignton with the Dartmouth Steam Railway. This is Kingswear Station, from which there is a ferry to Dartmouth

The Avocet Line

Of the surviving branch railways, the 15 km (9 1/2 mile) long 'Avocet Line' from Exeter to Exmouth via Topsham and Lympstone is the busiest branch in the West of England, boasting 1.7 million travellers per year in 2013. Regular commuter traffic is greatly boosted in summer by tourists and day trippers. Running parallel to the Avocet Line is the Exe Estuary Trail, which will be a marathon length 42 km/26 mile cycle and walkway when completed.

The Riviera Line

Like Exmouth, Torquay and Paignton owe much of their development and consequently their architectural heritage to the railway. They remain connected to the national network via Newton Abbot, Paignton being the terminus of the 'Riviera Line'. Passengers can continue their railway journey to Kingswear and take the ferry to Dartmouth by transferring to the splendidly scenic Dartmouth Steam Railway (page 22).

The Tarka Line

Devon's longest surviving branch is the North Devon line. Running from Exeter to Barnstaple, it was renamed the 'Tarka Line' after *Tarka the Otter:* its author Henry Williamson lived in Georgeham near Barnstaple between the world wars and wrote the novel there.

For much of its route the Tarka Line follows the beautiful valleys of the Creedy, Yeo and Taw. With thirteen stations there are ample opportunities to stop and enjoy the countryside or participate in the accompanying Rail Ale Trail, which tempts travellers with eighteen participating pubs.

From Coleford Junction, just beyond Yeoford, the line of the former Southern Railway branched westwards taking the *Atlantic Express* to Padstow and also providing an alternative route to Plymouth when storms closed the line between Dawlish and Teignmouth. It survives as the 'Withered Arm' as far as Okehampton and has been the subject of recent debate over a possible expansion of services. At the time of writing (2017), network trains to Okehampton are confined to some Sunday Rover services. From Okehampton passengers may (at present) take connecting Dartmoor Railway trains on to Meldon (page 24), whilst special events use the line to Coleford Junction.

Tamar Valley Line

The beautiful Tamar Valley Line runs for 22km (14 miles) from Plymouth to Gunnislake, a former mining village high on the Cornish bank of the river. The line was built in 1090 as part of the Southern Railway route from Exeter to Plymouth via Okehampton. Although the continuation of the branch to Callington was closed in 1965 and the main line truncated at Okehampton in 1968, the Tamar Valley line remains a vital service for local communities.

In its early years, the line carried minerals from the Tamar Valley's mines. As mining declined in the late 19th and early 20th centuries, market garden produce from the Tamar Valley's sheltered and fertile fields gave the railways more business. Fresh produce, especially early daffodils and strawberries, were rushed to markets all over Britain. Plymothians soon discovered the charms of taking a day's excursion up the Tamar Valley by rail. Sunday school treats and strawberry teas became an institution.

As well as a Rail Ale Trail similar to that on the Tarka Line, there are

Yeoford Station on the Tarka Line, which runs from Exeter to Barnstaple and is 63 km (39 miles) long

The Calstock Viaduct on the Tamar Valley Line, which provides an excellent day out

several attractive features along the Tamar Valley Line. Passengers gain a memorable worm's eye view of both Brunel's Royal Albert Bridge and its neighbour, the 1961 road bridge. Equally impressive is the Calstock Viaduct. Designed by Richard Church, it was completed in 1907 with 12,000 concrete blocks. Its twelve arches of 18 m (60 ft) span carry the Tamar Valley Line 36 m (118 ft) above the water.

At the splendidly restored and maintained Bere Ferrers station is the Tamar Belle Visitor Centre (page 30).

Buckfastleigh Station on the South Devon Railway. Number 5526 is a Class 4575 2-6-2 T built in 1928 by the GWR

Preserved railways and stations

Devon has a number of preserved railways and stations where vintage locomotives, carriages and rolling stock are complemented by a wealth of period detail. Set amid superb natural scenery, they allow visitors to step back in time and owe much of their interest to the fact that they are not static museums, but heritage in action. Visitors come aboard and experience the distinctive sights, sounds and smells of earlier rail travel.

South Devon Railway, Buckfastleigh-Totnes

The South Devon Railway follows the old Great Western Railway's branch line along the beautiful Dart Valley for seven miles from Totnes to Buckfastleigh. Opened in 1872, the branch was closed to all trains in 1962. It was reopened as the Dart Valley Railway in 1969, thus preserving Buckfastleigh and Staverton stations. Although the last 3 km of track to Ashburton were lost to road improvements on the A38 in 1971, the line has gained a new station at Totnes. Built with rescued GWR materials, it complements the nearby mainline station.

As well as a considerable fleet of steam locomotives, mainly GWR stock, the railway has a variety of mainline and industrial diesels. Its oldest exhibit is *Tiny*, an 0-4-0WT broad gauge locomotive. Built in 1868, *Tiny* is preserved in the Buckfastleigh station museum, which presents a vivid picture of the Ashburton branch throughout its life from the broad gauge era to the present day. Exhibits include track, signalling, photographs, tools and a fascinating collection of Victorian paintings showing the construction of the South Devon main line, including the atmospheric system with its pipes and pumping houses (see page 8).

Many of the railway's carriages and wagons are also pre-1948 GWR stock, restored to prime condition. Typically, these are side corridor compartment coaches with moquette upholstery.

As with Devon's other heritage railways, everything *works*. Take time to view the signal boxes with their levers and wires operating the points and signals; watch the drivers watering their engines or exchanging tokens with the signalmen and see the engineers at work restoring locomotives or rolling stock at the Buckfastleigh workshop.

Buckfastleigh station TQ11 0DZ,, signed from A38. (0843) 357 1420 or (01364) 644370

Engineers at work at the Buckfastleigh Station workshop

'Lydham Manor' steaming towards Churston on the Dartmouth Steam Railway. Sparks from the engine have scorched the embankment

Dartmouth Steam Railway

The railway reached Paignton in 1859 and was extended to Kingswear in 1864. Closed beyond Paignton in 1972, it was reopened as what is now the Dartmouth Steam Railway, which follows the spectacularly beautiful coastal and riverside track from Paignton to Kingswear.

Part of the main network between 1864 and 1972, this called for impressive engineering works. As well as deep cuttings and lengthy embankments, engineers were obliged to build the 106 m (116 yd) long Broadsands (Hookhills) Viaduct and the 454 m (495 yd) long Greenway Tunnel – all in only 10.8 km (6.7 miles).

Starting from Queen's Park station, an independent station built next to the main Paignton station, passengers can alight at Goodrington and Churston stations, as well as the new Greenway Halt to visit Greenway (National Trust), crime writer Agatha Christie's summer home. From the Kingswear terminus, a ferry takes passengers over to Dartmouth's Station Restaurant. Painted in GWR colours, the restaurant was the only station in England without track.

Just outside Kingswear Station, heading for Paignton

Kingswear station, restored like all the stations on the line in period GWR style, has been a favoured location for films including *The French Lieutenant's Woman*. The former Royal Dart Hotel next to the station and slipway is part of the station's history. Originally the Plume of Feathers, it changed its name to the Station Hotel when the railway arrived and retains its Italianate station clock marked 'GWR'.

The gas works, coal wagons and sidings that once lined the quay beside Kingswear station have long been replaced by a marina. Rail passengers no longer board ocean going ships from Dartmouth, but many do board the Dartmouth Steam Railway's fleet of boats, including the paddle steamer Kingswear Castle, which ply the river Dart and the adjacent coast. Run in conjunction with the company's buses (many of them open top), they offer a variety of travel possibilities. Particularly popular are the Round Robin Trips combining rail travel to Kingswear, river boat to Totnes and bus back to Paignton; or vice versa.

Paignton Station, TQ4 6AF, signed from town centre. (01803) 555872

Dartmoor Railway

The Dartmoor Railway (part of the Southern Railway which linked London Waterloo with Plymouth) is centred on restored Okehampton station, the main station on the 25 km (15.5 mile) long line from Meldon in the west to Coleford Junction on the Tarka Line in the east. At the time of writing, some trains hauled by vintage diesels were available on the 4 km (2.5 mile) route from Okehampton to Meldon, whilst special events use the line to Coleford Junction..

Okehampton station was opened in 1871 and became a junction for lines to Padstow and Bude as well as Plymouth – the line west being made possible by Meldon and Lake Viaducts in 1874. These triumphs of Victorian engineering over challenging terrain are now used by the Granite Way, a cycle/walkway that follows the railway towards Lydford and forms part of Cycle Route 27 (page 39).

After the 1963 Beeching Report, the Bude line was closed and the Exeter-Plymouth line was cut back to Meldon Quarry, where stone for railway ballast helped its survival until closure in 2011. In 1997 a Youth Hostel opened in the former goods shed at Okehampton, whilst the station was restored in Southern Railway livery and style, with evocative details such as luggage barrows, leather suitcases and railway posters. Okehampton station also offers a pleasant buffet and a railway shop.

Okehampton Station, EX20 1EA. Phone (01837) 55164 for details of opening times and current services.

Steaming into Launceston station aboard 'Lillian', an 1883 Hunslet

Launceston Steam Railway

Launceston Steam Railway is just over the border in Cornwall. It has preserved 4 km (2 ½ miles) of trackbed along the lovely Kensey Valley on the old North Cornwall Railway. Part of the LSWR system, this ran from Halwill Junction in Devon to Padstow in Cornwall, crossing the Tamar just east of Launceston, which it reached in 1886 – although the GWR line to Launceston from Tavistock had arrived earlier, in 1865.

Four Hunslet steam locomotives, dating from the 1883 to 1901, take passengers from Launceston station via Hunt's Crossing halt to Newmills station with its recreational facilities. Built in Leeds, the Hunslets originally worked in the slate quarries of North Wales. They were restored by Launceston Steam Railway, which also built or adapted all their carriages and wagons based on traditional designs, as well as building the station on a site different from the old GWR and LSWR stations. To do this they used material, including the LSWR canopy and cast iron columns, from a variety of sources. The station has a gift and bookshop with an extensive range of railway titles. There is also a large collection of vintage cars, vans and motorbikes.

Launceston PL15 8DA (01566) 775665.

Plym Valley Railway

The Plym Valley Railway has a varied collection of restored locomotives, carriages and wagons. Its events programme features a variety of steam and diesel locomotives, including *Albert*, a 0-4-0ST built by Andrew Barclay at Kilmarnock in 1948 and 0-4-0ST *Merlin*, built in 1939.

These locomotives haul vintage restored coaches including BR Mark II's along 2.4 km (1.5 miles) of attractively wooded track from Marsh Mills near Plymouth to Plym Bridge. The PVR has rebuilt both this section of track, including Lee Moor Crossing and two bridges, whilst repairing a third bridge. It also rebuilt Marsh Mills station and the halt at Plym Bridge, which was re-opened in 2012 fifty years after the line was closed in 1962.

The line is the lower section of the South Devon & Tavistock Railway (later a GWR branch line) that was opened to Tavistock in 1859, with a link to Launceston in 1865. Like the Tamar Valley Line (page 18), it carried minerals and stone from nearby mines and quarries and was also popular with day trippers from Plymouth. Its course to Plym Bridge and along the Plym Valley to near Clearbrook is now a cycle/walkway and part of the traffic-free Drake's Trail (page 39) to Tavistock.

From Marsh Mills roundabout near Plymouth take Plympton exit and follow signs. Plym Valley Railway PL7 4NW (01752) 330881

Opposite: Milk churns and leather luggage at Marsh Mills

Above: 'Albert' pulling BR Mark II carriages, built at Derby in 1967

Below: An 08 diesel shunter built in 1952, one of the oldest British shunters in working order

Seaton Tramway

This 5 km (3 mile) long electric tramway links Seaton with Colyford and Colyton along the scenic Axe valley, noted for its bird life. Opened in 1971, the tramway employs a section of the old Southern Railway branch line from Seaton Junction that operated from 1868 to 1963.

It features a variety of trams running on 2 ft 9 in (0.84 m) track, drawing power from overhead cables. Some of the fleet was built in the early 20th century. Car 14 is the oldest, dating from 1904, whilst Car 16, an open-topped Bournemouth tram, was rebuilt at Seaton. Other trams at Seaton were constructed much later for heritage tramways. Numbers 9, 10 and 11, for example, were built at Bolton and Seaton based on design elements of the old Plymouth and Blackburn trams.

Car 19 is of special local interest. Constructed in 1906, a year after Exeter's first tram went into service, it ran in the city until buses replaced trams in 1931. Bought by Seaton Tramway in 1994, it needed four years' careful restoration to bring it to its present condition, and is the only Exeter tram to be preserved.

Follow signs in Seaton to Harbour Road car park. EX24 6HA
(01297) 20375

*Opposite:
Car 16,
originally a
Bournemouth
open top car,
rebuilt at
Seaton for wet
weather use*

*Top right:
Car 14, the
oldest in the
fleet*

*Middle:
Car 10, newly
built based on
design
elements from
both Plymouth
and Blackburn
trams*

*Bottom:
Car 8, built in
Eastbourne in
1968 specially
for the Seaton
2ft 9in gauge*

Tamar Belle, Bere Ferrers

Bere Ferrers station on the Tamar Valley Line retains its original stationmaster's house and booking hall and has a host of period details from vintage bicycles to hanging baskets and lampposts. It is also home to the Tamar Belle Heritage Centre, whose attractions include a 1920s LNER passenger coach and two wagons, plus operational diesel shunting locomotives giving sample rides recreating the types of train that ran on the branch line. Among these, the blue Hunslet locomotive worked at Ernesettle sidings (just down the line) until the 1970s.

Refreshments are offered in a 1960s dining/buffet coach and en suite B & B accommodation in teak carriages dating from the 1920s.

On site and operational is the 1927 turntable from Devonport Dockyard. The 1900 Stothert & Pitt goods yard crane, formerly at Tavistock North station, is hand cranked and also in working order. Tamar Belle's 1876 signal box was rescued from Pinhoe station on the former Southern main line near Exeter complete with its Victorian Stevens lever frame and block instruments. Wired to a computer simulator, this sends and receives 'phantom' trains so long as the correct sequence of signalling operations is given – a wonderful 'hands on' railway experience.

Bere Ferrers station PL20 7LT (07813) 360066.

Devon Railway Centre at Bickleigh

The Devon Railway Centre is based around Bickleigh station on the old Exe Valley Line from Exeter to Dulverton. Opened in 1885, Bickleigh was closed with the rest of the line in 1963 by Dr Beeching. It became another sad, derelict railway site until the Giquel family began restoration in 1997. Bickleigh's station house and engine shed, both of characteristic railway design and quality, have been restored to prime condition. Track has been laid around the site and visitors enjoy unlimited rides on the narrow and miniature gauge railways.

Narrow gauge carriages are hauled by *Rebecca*, an O & K (Orenstein and Koppel) locomotive built in Berlin in 1912, or by the steam outline diesels *Ivor* and *Horatio*. There are many other locomotives besides, including *Claude*, built in 1959 for North Devon Clay at Great Torrington and formerly part of Seaton Tramway's collection.

The centre's model railway layouts are housed in restored 1950s coaches, painted in GWR cream and chocolate. Each layout is controlled by its own push button. The period detail in these models is remarkable, not only on the locomotives and carriages, but also the 'extras', from houses and people to vintage cars and trams. The centre is packed with railway memorabilia too, from evocative railway posters to wheelbarrows, leather trunks and milk churns.

Devon Railway Centre EX16 8RG (01884) 855671.

Lynton & Barnstaple Railway

One of the country's highest narrow gauge lines, the Lynton & Barnstaple Railway was completed in 1898 and did much to popularise North Devon with holidaymakers before closure in 1935. Today, visitors enjoy 3 km (2 mile) round trips with fine views of Exmoor on a restored section from Woody Bay station.

Woody Bay has been restored in Southern Railway style, complete with all the delightful period paraphernalia of art deco posters, red fire buckets and leather luggage. Photo displays in the goods brake van (built in Barnstaple, 1908) describe the history of the railway and how it has been restored. Teas, light refreshments, books, DVDs and railway souvenirs are on sale in the station.

Journeys are steam hauled, principally by *Isaac*, a 1953 Bagnall locomotive built for the South African Rustenberg Platinum Mine, or *Axe*, a side and well tank locomotive built for the French government in 1915 by Kerr Stuart of Stoke-on-Trent. Visitors travel in restored Victorian carriages which originally served on the Lynton & Barnstaple Railway. Other vintage rolling stock includes an observation car built in Bristol, 1898.

The railway's industrial rolling stock includes box cars, brake vans and open wagons. It has a Bagley and two Hunslet diesel locomotives serving as works trains. Along with MOD flat bed wagons they are used for track maintenance and construction. Further extensions and restoration of the Lynton to Barnstaple line are planned for the future.

*Opposite:
The restored
line runs
through
north Devon's
glorious
scenery*

*Top right:
Locomotive
'Axe', built
in Stoke-on-
Trent in 1915*

*Bottom right:
Woody Bay
Station,
lovingly
restored in
Southern
Railway style*

Further down the railway's former course between Goodleigh and Bratton Fleming is the magnificent Chelfham Viaduct (SS 608357) which is the largest narrow gauge railway bridge in Britain, 121 m (367 ft) long and 23 m (75 ft) high. It was designed by Frank W Chanter and constructed of cream coloured Marland brick with blue brick bands at the springing of the arches and at rail level.

Woody Bay Station, EX31 4RA (01598) 763487

33

Lynton Cliff Railway

Lynton's unique Cliff Railway was built in 1890 in response to North Devon's burgeoning tourist industry and the long-standing problem of bringing food, coal and other essentials up the steep slope from Lynmouth's quays to Lynton. Designed by George Croydon Marks, it was largely financed by wealthy publisher Sir George Newnes, who also backed the narrow gauge Lynton & Barnstaple Railway (page 32). It works on simple and entirely ecological principles by balancing the weight of its two cars on a pulley system.

The top car's tank is filled with water fed in from the West Lyn via a pipe, enabling it to descend and thus pull the lighter car at the bottom 261m (862ft) up the inclined plane, a rise of 152m (500ft) on a 58% gradient. When the first car reaches the bottom, it dumps its load of 3200 litres (700 gallons) of water. Capable of carrying up to forty passengers, the railway has been in continuous service since first built.

North Walk, Lynton, and Lynmouth sea front. 01598 753908.

Babbacombe Cliff Railway

Babbacombe's cliff railway to Oddicombe beach was opened in 1926. George Marks, who had designed the Lynton and Lynmouth Cliff Railway as well as engineering funicular cliff railways at Saltburn, Bridgnorth, Clifton and Abersytwyth, was consultant.

The vertical drop is half that of the Lynton and Lynmouth railway, 76m (250ft), though its length is not greatly shorter at 220m (720ft), giving it a much gentler 35% gradient. *01803 328750.*

Opposite:
Lynton Cliff
Railway

Right:
Babbacombe
Cliff Railway.
An excellent
visitor centre
gives a full
explanation

Instow signal box

Exploring Devon's railway heritage on foot or by bike

Tarka Trail

Over 48 km (30 miles) of North Devon's former railway track is incorporated in the 300 km (180 mile) Tarka Trail linking Dartmoor with the North Devon coast and Exmoor. From Braunton to Barnstaple; round the Taw/Torridge estuary to Instow and Bideford and thence south to Great Torrington and Meeth, the Trail is all on disused railway and open to both cyclists and walkers. It has three places of particular railway interest.

Instow's signal box, built in 1872, is preserved as it was when the railway closed, with its levers, a short section of re-laid track and a working signal. It is open to the public on occasional Sundays and Bank Holidays.

Instow Quay

Bideford's Railway Heritage Centre includes the preserved station buildings and a working replica of the original signal box with memorabilia. A 1942 parcels van houses railway exhibits and period photographs, whilst refreshments are offered in a coach. The centre also has a Planet diesel and a BR standard brake van.

East-the-Water, Bideford

Great Torrington's former station house is now the Puffing Billy pub. A vintage carriage, wagons and a diesel locomotive stand on a short section of track by the platform and are open to view on Thursdays.

B3227 on western fringe of Great Torrington.

Cycles can be hired at several points along the trail, including Braunton, Barnstaple, Fremington Quay, Bideford and Great Torrington.

Christow Station

Christow's former station is owned by a railway enthusiast and stands beside the B3212 cycling route at SX 839868. The sidings date from 1882, when the Heathfield-Ashton section of the Teign Valley Railway opened to goods traffic, although the line did not reach Exeter until 1903. The Exeter & Teign Valley Railway was mainly a branch line carrying minerals, but sometimes took mainline trains when storms closed the coastal route via Teignmouth.

Christow has a variety of industrial rolling stock, including tipper wagons from Kingsteignton clay pits, two converted camping cars, box cars, flat bed wagons and a 1949 petrol driven gang trolley.

Follow B3212. Take Doddiscombsleigh turning. Turn left along track after 200 m. Exeter & Teign Valley Railway 01647 253108

Camping van interior at Christow Station

Haytor Tramway

The 29 km (18 mile) Templer Way footpath traces the route of Haytor Tramway (page 4) from Haytor quarries to Teigngrace and continues to Teignmouth. To explore the whole route Ordnance Survey Explorer maps 110 and OL28 are needed. The best extant sections are seen by following the granite rails towards Haytor Rocks from the parking area at SX768775 (OL28). Approaching from Bovey Tracey on the B3387, this is 100 m right along the minor road to Manaton. Follow the rails on to the old quarries west of Haytor Rocks, a distance of 2.5 km (1 1/2 miles). NB this is not a cyclepath.

www.devon.gov.uk/templerwayleaflet.pdf

Plymouth & Dartmoor Railway

The trackbed of the Plymouth & Dartmoor Railway (page 4) is best explored on foot or by bike from the car park by Princetown's High Moorland Visitor Centre (OL28, SX588735). Turn left out of the car park along the rough road. Just past the fire station bear left as signed on a narrow fenced path, which bears right. Go through a gate. The path widens to a gritty track, and passes a coniferous plantation to the railway embankment. An 8 km (5 mile) loop can be made following the trackbed around Foggintor, King Tor and Swelltor quarries and thence retracing your steps or wheel tracks to the start.

The looping line of the Plymouth & Dartmoor Railway

The Granite Way

Running parallel to the Dartmoor Railway from Okehampton station to Meldon for 3.75km (2.5 miles), the well surfaced Granite Way continues for 7.2km (4.5 miles). First, it crosses Meldon Viaduct, built in 1874; this cycle/walkway spans the West Okement for 162m (540ft) at a height of 36m (120ft). It continues over the multiple granite arches of Lake Viaduct to Southerly Halt with superb Dartmoor views en route. Beyond, lanes and sections of former railway track lead on to Lydford, Tavistock and, via the Drake Trail to the Plym Valley.

Plym Valley

Starting from Marsh Mills station, there is a good deal of railway heritage along the 17km (10 1/2 mile) Plym Valley cycle/walkway, including the 300m long Shaugh Tunnel and a series of viaducts. Built in 1905 of Staffordshire blue brick, Cann Viaduct replaced the original Brunel wooden viaduct of 1859 – the stone pillars of which remain.

The cycleway continues to Tavistock as part of the Drake's Trail, using other sections of the former railway en route. Along with the Tarka Trail, it forms part of the 158km (99 mile) long Cycle Route 27, linking Plymouth to Ilfracombe.

From Marsh Mills roundabout near Plymouth take Plympton exit and follow signs.

Wray Valley Trail

Bovey Tracey's Station House is the town's Heritage Centre, packed with local history displays including railway memorabilia and a 1930s GWR brake van built in Swindon. Start from here and walk or cycle the first two miles of the developing Wray Valley Trail on the former branch railway (1866-1959).

Bovey Tracey Station Road car park.
Bovey Heritage Centre: (01626) 835078

The Ruby Way

At Holsworthy, this cycle/footpath from Hatherleigh to Bude crosses the Derriton Viaduct. Built in 1898, it is 29 m (95 ft) high and comprises ten precast concrete arches made to look like stone.

Follow Bodmin Street out of Holsworthy towards Derriton.

The future of Devon's Railways

Passenger numbers increased year on year during the early 21st century. On Devon's main line, passenger journeys starting or ending at Exeter St David's rose from 1.53 million in 2002/03 to 2.51 million in 2014/15. Comparable figures for Plymouth are 1.43 million and 2.50 million, and Newton Abbot's figures rose from 0.64 million to 1.14 million. It seems likely this will continue, and that railways will again be vital to Devon's future.